an

GROS!

Kids Love To Sing!

BY: KEN CARDER

ILLUSTRATIONS: TAMMY ORTNER

About the Author KEN CARDER

Ken is a graduate of The University of Akron in Akron, OH with a B.A. in Communication And Rhetoric, and of Evangelical School of Theology in Myerstown, PA with a M.Div. For the past three years Ken has worked exclusively with Twin Sisters Productions to develop new educational music resources for children. Ken is the Children's Pastor at Community Church of Portage Lakes (Akron, OH). He and his wife, Tammy, have worked extensively with young children in churches, summer camps, schools, a syndicated radio ministry broadcast, and community theater. Ken and Tammy are proud parents of three children, Stephen, Nathan, and McKenna.

www.twinsisters.com
1-800-248-TWIN (8946)
Twin Sisters Productions, LLC • Akron, OH

Credits:
Publisher: Twin Sisters Productions, LLC
Executive Producers: Kim Mitzo Thompson, Karen Mitzo Hilderbrand
Music Arranged by: Hal Wright
Workbook Author: Ken Carder
Book Design: Angelee Randlett, Christine Della Penna
Illustrations: Tammy Ortner

ISBN-10 1575838702
ISBN-13 9781575838700

Acrobat Reader 6.0.1 system requirements
WINDOWS
- Intel® Pentium® processor
- Microsoft® Windows 98 Second Edition, Windows Millennium Edition, Windows NT® 4.0 with Service Pack 6, Windows 2000 with Service Pack 2, Windows XP Professional or Home Edition, Windows XP Tablet PC Edition
- 32MB of RAM (64MB recommended)
- 60MB of available hard-disk space
- Internet Explorer 5.01, 5.5, 6.0, or 6.1

MACINTOSH OS X v.10.2.2-10.3
- PowerPC® G3 processor
- Mac OS X v.10.2.2-10.3
- 32MB of RAM with virtual memory on (64MB recommended)
- 70MB of available hard-disk space

Acrobat Reader 5.1 system requirements
MACINTOSH OS 9.1-10.2.1
- PowerPC processor
- Mac OS 9.1, 9.2, or 9.2.2, or Mac OS X v.10.1.3, 10.1.5, or 10.2
- 64MB of RAM
- 30MB of available hard disk space (an additional 60 MB is needed temporarily during installation)
- HFS formatted hard drive
- Additional 70 MB of hard-disk space for Asian fonts (optional)
- Web browser support
- The Web browsers within which Adobe PDF files may be viewed are:
  Internet Explorer 5.0
  Netscape Navigator 4.5 to 4.77, 6.1
  America Online 6.0

Adobe Acrobat Reader Installation Instructions

WINDOWS
1. Insert CD into Drive.
2. Access CD by double-clicking "My Computer" on the desktop.
3. Open "PC Installer" folder.
4. Double-click "AdbeRdr60_enu_full.exe"
5. Follow Installation Instructions.

MACINTOSH OS X v.10.2.2-10.3
1. Insert CD into Drive.
2. Double-click on "PDF and Installers" Icon on the desktop.
3. Open "MAC Installer" folder.
4. Open "MacOS 10.2.2-10.3" folder.
5. Drag "Adobe Reader 6.0" folder to your hard drive.

MACINTOSH OS 9.1-10.2.1 (Acrobat Reader 5.1)
1. Insert CD into Drive.
2. Double-click on "PDF and Installers" Icon on the desktop.
3. Open "MAC Installer" folder.
4. Open "MacOS 9.1-10.2.1" folder.
5. Double-click on "Acrobat Reader Installer."
6. Click "Continue" when prompted.
7. Follow installation instructions.

INTRODUCTION

Most kids love the chance to be gross and disgusting. I've reached that conclusion after many years of summer camp ministries with children and middle-school kids. The opportunity to say or do something gross and revolting brings a freedom from kids' often boring days and predictable routines. It's exhilarating to do something you wouldn't normally do—and not be punished for it!

Enjoy the Gross and Not-So-Gross Songs at home, while on vacation, around a cozy family campfire or a not-so-cozy bonfire at the end of a day at summer camp! You'll be surprised how kids will laugh, groan, and sing along. Lead the singing without worrying about how awful you think you might sound—few kids or adults will sound any better. Just concentrate on creating a memory or two for kids! Print the lyrics on this enhanced CD from any computer. Make up additional verses or change a few words to customize the songs to your group experiences. The bottom line… have fun!

Toss out a few jokes and riddles between songs—the kids will groan and maybe beg you to stop. But the truth is they're smiling inside, begging you for more, and can't wait to tell the same joke to someone else!

Play Together! Some adults have concluded that kids today don't know how to have fun apart from their video games and competitive sports. Try a few of the large group field activities, the thinking games, the gross competitions, the stunts and experiments. Get kids up, moving, laughing, and playing together.

The Gross and Not-so-Gross Things To Make are ideas of easy crafts to do at home or camp. These are perfect for a rainy day, that downtime during the afternoon. Keep in mind that it's not the quality of the crafts that matter most. What matters is the interaction and relationship building—the memories that are being made. Most kids love Skits and Pranks. I've included some very old classic sketches and practical jokes that kids can do with very little rehearsal.

Gross Food—this is where most of the adults will bail out! I've selected recipes that might tug at your stomach and will certainly get a reaction from kids of all ages.

Caution: some of the games, activities, and recipes will need some adult supervision. Look for this symbol:

May you have a disgustingly beautiful time together with the kids you love! Remember, have fun and create a memory.

Ken Carder

1.
Why did the toilet paper roll down the hill?
Because it wanted to get to the bottom!

2.
How do you make a snake cry?
Take away its rattle!

3.
What monkey can fly?
A hot air baboon!

4.
What happened to the mouse who fell into a glass of soda?
Nothing, it was a soft drink!

5.
Why did the firefly get bad grades in school?
He wasn't very bright!

6.
Why do birds fly south?
It's too far to walk!

7.
Why did the boy bring toilet paper to the birthday party?
Because he's a party pooper!

8.
What's worse than finding a worm in your apple?
Finding half a worm!

9.
What is a dog's favorite snack?
Pupcorn

10.
Why don't elephants pick their nose?
They don't know where to hide a 30-pound booger!

11.
Why did the booger cross the road?
Because he was tired of getting picked on.

12.
How do you count cows?
With a cowculator

Groaners
Jokes Kids Love To Tell

13.
What did the chicken say to the farmer?
Nothing! A chicken can't talk!

14.
Why did the fish cross the river?
To get to its school!

15.
What is a volcano?
A mountain with hiccups!

16.
Why does a hummingbird hum?
It doesn't know the words!

17.
Where do you find a dog with no legs?
Right where you left him!

18.
How do you make a tissue dance?
Put a little boogie in it!

19.
Why does a gorilla have big nostrils?
Because it has big fingers!

20.
Why didn't the skeleton cross the road?
Because he had no body to go with!

21.
What is Beethoven doing in his grave?
Decomposing!

22.
What is the difference between boogers & broccoli?
Kids don't eat broccoli

23.
What do rabbits do when they get married?
Go on a bunnymoon

24.
What do you call a sleeping bull?
A bulldozer!

FAKE WOUNDS

Bring out a scream with one or more fake wounds and a great story!

You'll need:
- Petroleum jelly
- Toothpick
- Bowl
- Red food coloring
- A white tissue
  - Powdered cocoa

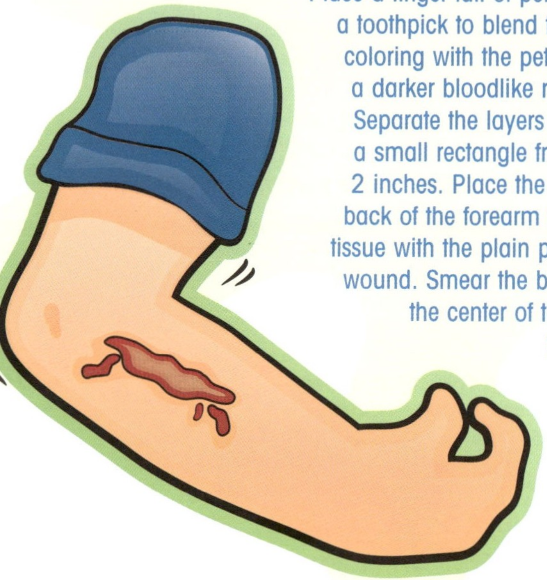

Place a finger-full of petroleum jelly into a bowl. Use a toothpick to blend three or four drops of red food coloring with the petroleum jelly. To make the color a darker bloodlike red, blend in a pinch of cocoa. Separate the layers of a facial tissue, then rip out a small rectangle from one layer about 3 inches by 2 inches. Place the tissue at your wound site (the back of the forearm is a good spot). First, cover the tissue with the plain petroleum jelly, molding a gooey wound. Smear the blood-colored petroleum jelly in the center of the wound, sprinkle cocoa onto the edges, and rub the cocoa in to make the edges dark. Now go show someone! Be prepared with a sad tale or spine-tingling story, too!

Experiments & Stunts

NATURAL GAS

Wow your friends by inflating a balloon using natural gas!
It's not what you're thinking!

You'll need:
- One packet of yeast (available in the grocery store)
- A small, clean, clear, plastic soda bottle
- 1 teaspoon of sugar
- Warm water
- Small balloon

Fill the bottle with about one inch of warm water. Add all of the yeast and gently swirl the bottle a few seconds. Add the sugar and swirl it around some more. As the yeast absorbs the sugar, it creates a GAS—carbon dioxide. Put the neck of the balloon over the top of the bottle and allow the bottle to sit for awhile in a warm place. Soon the balloon should start to blow up because it is filling with the gas created by the living yeast! When you've amazed your friends, remove the balloon and throw it away. Pour out the yeast solution in the sink. What does it smell like?

PAPER CLIP FLOAT

Don't eat or drink this float—hold out for the rootbeer float from your favorite ice cream hangout. But challenge your friends to make a paper clip float!

You'll need:
- Clean, dry paper clips
- Toilet tissue paper
- A bowl of water
- Pencil with eraser

Fill the bowl with water, and place a paper clip on top of the water. The paper clip will sink. Let others try, then gently drop one sheet of toilet tissue paper flat onto the surface of the water. Now, carefully place a dry paper clip flat on top of the tissue. Use the eraser end of the pencil to carefully poke the tissue—not the paper clip—until the tissue sinks. With some luck, the tissue will sink and leave the paper clip floating!

Gross & Not-So-Gross
Experiments & Stunts

RAISING RAISINS

Put a few raisins into a bottle of clear soda and watch them rise and shimmy like they've come to life!

You'll need:
- A bottle of clear soda
- Raisins

The irregular surfaces of raisins hold some carbon dioxide from the carbonation in the soda, and when enough bubbles accumulate, they lift raisins to the surface.

STALK SHOW

You'll need:
- Celery stalk or white cut flowers
- Red food coloring
- Tall, clear jar
- Water

Pour water in a tall, clear jar and add the red food coloring. Stand a stalk of celery in the glass. Wait 24 hours, and the celery leaves will turn red. This will work, too, with white flowers. In a process called osmosis, the plants absorb the water—and the coloring—and carry it to the leaves.

 # LIGHTNING SPARKS

You'll need:
- Modeling clay
- Large metal paper clips
- Inflated balloon
- Wool sweater

Make a sculpture out of modeling clay, inserting several large metal paper clips somewhere into the design. Take the sculpture into a dark room or closet, and rub an inflated balloon against a wool sweater for 30 seconds. Hold the balloon close to, —but not touching—the paper clip. Sparks should jump between the balloon and the paper clips. Try rubbing the balloon against your hair, too.

 # RUBBER EGGS

Make a quivering, rubbery egg sac!

You'll need:
- An egg
- Glass jar
- Vinegar

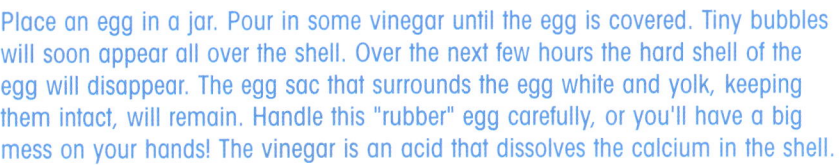

Place an egg in a jar. Pour in some vinegar until the egg is covered. Tiny bubbles will soon appear all over the shell. Over the next few hours the hard shell of the egg will disappear. The egg sac that surrounds the egg white and yolk, keeping them intact, will remain. Handle this "rubber" egg carefully, or you'll have a big mess on your hands! The vinegar is an acid that dissolves the calcium in the shell.

QUICK CHANGE ARTIST

Demonstrate your power over the natural elements, changing colors at your command!

You'll need
- 1/4 cup grape juice
- Small, clear glass
- 1 Tablespoon of baking soda
- 1 Tablespoon of white vinegar

Pour the grape juice into the glass. Slowly mix the baking soda into the grape juice. The color at the top of the juice will change to blue. Now add the vinegar to the mixture, a drop at a time; the color will change to pink where the vinegar drips. Pour out the liquid in the sink and notice how dark it becomes.

Grape juice looks purple because its molecules are arranged in such a way that it absorbs all the colors of light except purple. Adding other substances changes the molecular structure of grape juice, so its color changes.

EGG IN A BOTTLE

How do you get a shelled, hard-boiled egg into a narrow-necked bottle without damaging the egg? Easy!

You'll need:
- Cooking oil, butter, or margarine
- An eight-ounce glass baby bottle
- Two small, shelled, hard-boiled eggs
- A piece of paper, four inches square
- Matches
- Adult supervision

Rub the oil, butter, or margarine around the inside of the mouth of the bottle. Fold the paper to form an accordion. Carefully light one end of the paper with a match, and drop it into the bottle. Quickly place the egg onto the mouth of the bottle. You did it!

PET WORM

You'll need:
- Glass jar with lid
- Soil, sand, leaves
- Dark paper
- One or two worms

A worm farm is fascinating! Put layers of soil, sand, and leaves in the bottom of a medium-sized glass jar. Place one or two worms on top of the leaves. Wrap the jar with paper to keep it dark. Remove the paper in several days and observe the changes.

BARKING SEALS!

With a little practice, you'll be able to get this simple looking experiment to sound like barking seals have invaded your house.

You'll need:
- Several paper cups—a variety of sizes, styles
- Several toothpicks
- Water
- Yarn
- Scissors
- Pencil

Cut off several pieces of yarn, each one a different length. Soak the yarn pieces in water for several minutes. While the yarn is soaking, take a paper cup and poke a small hole right in the middle of the bottom using a sharp pencil. Take a piece of the wet yarn and carefully push one end through the hole in the bottom of the cup. Tightly tie the end in the cup around the middle of a toothpick. Drop the toothpick into the cup so that it lies flat on the bottom of the cup—you may have to break off some of the toothpick until it fits. Wet your fingers, tightly pinch the yarn between your thumb and forefinger just below the cup, and pull down—hard. If you have trouble making a sound, add more water to the yarn and/or your fingers. Experiment with different lengths of yarn. Try a different kind of cup—maybe use a foam cup or a tiny paper bathroom cup. Notice any differences?

Pulling your fingers down the length of the yarn causes the yarn to vibrate. The vibrations travel up the yarn and into the cup; the cup and the air inside the cup vibrate, too.

Gross & Not-So-Gross
Games

GROSS EATING CONTEST

Ahead of time, fill two paper grocery bags with food items that smell or feel gross—nothing spoiled! Each bag must have the same items. Suggestions: raw onions, cold beans, cooked spaghetti, hardboiled eggs, black olives, cheese chunks, and lunchmeat. Divide your friends or family members into two teams. The first player on each team takes one item from the bag, eats it completely, and then passes the bag to the next player. The first team to eat all the food items in the bag is the winner!

SODA ROULETTE

You'll need a can of soda for each player. Vigorously shake one can of soda. Mix the cans up. Each player chooses a can, puts it up to his nose, and on the count of three opens it! Who is the unlucky winner?

MAGIC NUMBER

The object of the game is to force a player to say the Magic Number. To play, first choose a magic number—almost any number that you can count to quickly! On your turn, say only one OR two numbers next in the sequence. For example, say the magic number is 20. Player one counts "One, Two." The next player may say, "Three, Four." The next player may say, "Five." Play continues until a player is forced to say 20, the Magic Number. That player is out of the game. Continue playing until a champion is named! This game requires concentration and forward thinking!

15

PIG

You and a small group of friends will quickly pass the time with this classic game of strategy and chance.

You'll need:
- A die
- Paper
- Pencil

Take turns rolling a die and adding up your points. You can roll as many times as you want, but if you roll a 1, you lose all your points for that turn. When you choose to stop, write your score and pass the die to the next player. The first player to reach 100 points wins.

ADULT CANDY THROW UP

Most of your friends know what it feels like to have eaten too much candy! But do they know what their favorite candies look like when they've …let's say, come back up? Ahead of time, ask an adult to help you melt 6-10 candy bars in individual cupcake or muffin liners in a microwave. (Be certain to write down what candy bar you melted in each container!) Players pass and smell each container of candy throw-up and write down what name brand candy product they believe was "regurgitated."

For even more disgusting fun, put the melted candies in disposable diapers. Your friends must smell each diaper and guess what candy the baby passed!

16

Gross & Not-So-Gross

Games

MIND READER

One of your friends must think of a person, place, or thing! You must read her mind! You can only ask questions that she can answer by saying "yes" or "no." How many questions will you have to ask? Now, it's your turn to think of a person, place, or thing and your friend's turn to ask questions.

BEAT THE BUNNY

The object of the game is for the farmer to catch the bunny. No, we're not talking about a real farmer trapping a real bunny! This is a really fast game to play with a group of friends. You'll need two balls of different sizes. Players sit on the floor in a circle. Begin passing the bunny—the small ball—from player to player around the circle. When the bunny is about half way around, start passing the farmer—the large ball—in the same direction. Can players pass the farmer fast enough to catch up with the bunny? For more challenging play, the farmer can change directions, but the bunny can only go one way.

17

ODDS/EVENS

Play this game with another friend when you have a few minutes to spare. (This is great fun while waiting for your food at a sit-down restaurant—just don't get too loud!) One of you chooses to be "odds" and the other chooses to be "evens." Both of you make a fist, shake it, say, "One, two, three...shoot," and stick out one or two fingers. Count the fingers that are sticking out. If the total is an odd number, the player who picked odds wins that number of points; and the same goes for evens. The first player to reach 50 points wins.

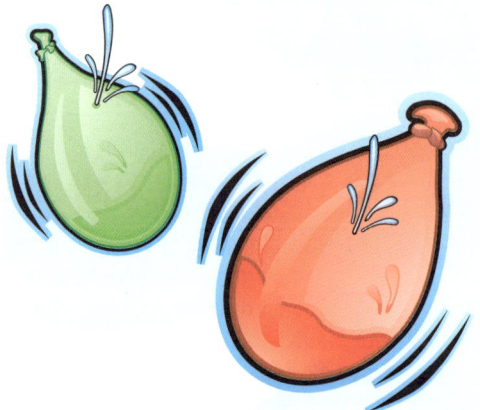

FAST TALKER

Now you can prove who in your group of friends talks too much! Challenge each friend to talk non-stop for one minute about a subject you choose. It's harder than you think! If the player hesitates or stops talking he is out of the game. You'll need someone with a watch or stopwatch to time each player. For more challenging play, have two friends talk at the same time about that topic for one minute.

WATER TIME BOMB

Poke a hole in a balloon before filling it with water. Now the water balloon is a time bomb with a slow leak. Players stand in a circle and toss the balloon around. The object is not to be the one holding the balloon when it runs out of water.

PUTT, PUTT GOLF

Miniature golfing every day may be out of the question! But here is a fun, inexpensive way to practice your game at home or at a restaurant while you wait for your food to arrive!

You'll need:
- Plain paper
- Markers, crayons
- Blindfolds—if you don't trust players to close their eyes!

Use a large sheet of copy paper or construction paper. Draw the fairway—an odd, oblong shape. At one end draw a line for the tee (or starting point). At the far end of the fairway draw a small circle—this is the hole! Now, place a marker, crayon, or pencil down at the tee, close your eyes, and try to draw a line to the hole! Open your eyes and lift the marker; that's your shot. Add a stroke if you strayed outside the boundaries. The next player then tees off on the same sheet. Play again, beginning where your last stroke ended. Your score is the number of shots it takes you to reach the hole. Play nine holes or even 18 like the pros.

WORMS IN A PIE

You'll need gummy worms, whipped cream, and aluminum pie plates or deep disposable plates—one for each person playing the game. Place the same amount of gummy worms on each plate and cover them with whipped cream. Blindfold each player. On the count of three, each player dips into the pie with their mouth, trying to pull out as many worms as they can. See who can pull out the most worms in a time limit or just set a certain amount of worms to find. For more fun, and if everyone is willing, put all the gummy worms and whipped cream in one large container and let players search together.

TEENY-TINY SCAVENGER HUNT

Send your friends outside in search of as many different natural items as they can find that fit in a small, plastic condiment container. Consider awarding points for each unique item collected, and extra points for live creatures that will be returned to nature, of course! If you go to a park be certain you have permission to disturb or remove natural items from the grounds.

SOCK WRESTLING

Mark off a small play area. Players take off their shoes, but leave on their socks and move around the ring. The idea of the game is for players to somehow remove a sock from their opponents. It can be played one-on-one or with several players in the ring at the same time. Players who lose both socks must leave the ring.

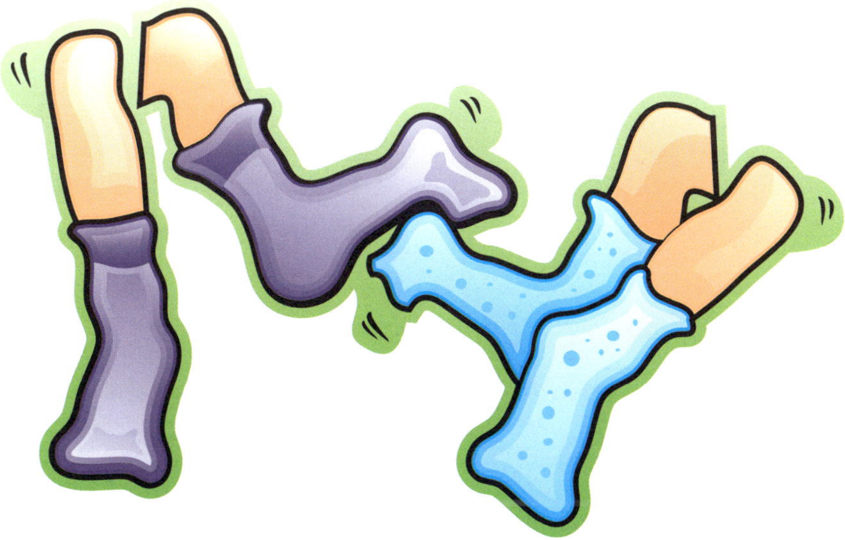

21

NAUSEATING NATURE HUNT

Make a list of icky items and the points that will be earned for each item that is found. Take a grocery bag and go out into the yard to find the items. Whoever gets the most points, wins.

Icky Items May Include:
- A dead moth
- Spoonful of tree sap
- Daddy long-legs
- Green caterpillar guts
- Squished berries
- A four-leaf clover
- A live slug
- A live worm
- Ants
- Moss
- Stinkweed
- A dead fly
- Snake
- Cricket

SPUD

Gather your friends together, everyone touching home base, and have each player count off. One player who is "It" throws a ball high in the air and calls out one player's number. As the other players scatter, the called player catches the ball and shouts, "Spud!" The other players must immediately freeze. The ball holder takes two giant steps toward any player, and tries to hit that player with the ball. The target person can try to dodge the ball by moving his body but not his feet. If the thrower misses OR the target catches the ball, the thrower earns an S. If he hits the target, that person earns an S. Whoever earns the letter becomes the next "It" and begins the next round. Players are eliminated once they earn S-P-U-D.

FLASHLIGHT SIGNALS

Play this game outside after dark with a large group of friends. Every player will need a flashlight! To begin, pair off with another friend, and create your own unique flashlight signal—for example, one short and one long flash followed by three short flashes. The partners separate and go to opposite ends of a large playing area. Each pair tries to reunite as quickly as possible by sending flashlight signals to each other. The first pair to reunite is the winner.

BLANKET STAND

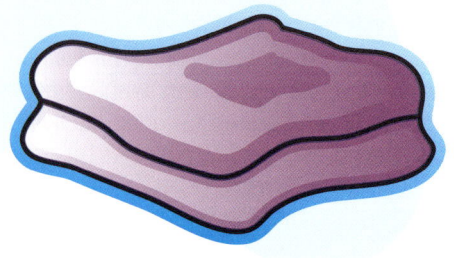

Spread out a blanket on the floor. The object of the game is to have your entire group of friends on the blanket so that no arms, legs, or other body parts are touching the ground off the blanket. If this is too easy, have your friends get off the blanket, fold the blanket in half, and try again. Keep folding the blanket in half! Soon, you'll end up in a big pile! Guaranteed!

24

SPITBALL TARGET PRACTICE

You'll never want to play darts again after using spit-wads instead! First, make a target on a piece of poster board, like a dartboard with circles and points marked off. (Of course, with permission, you might draw your dartboard on a sliding glass door using dry-erase or washable markers.) Next, each player must make his arsenal of spitballs. Give each player a different color piece of paper. Each player shreds the paper into small pieces, wets them in his mouth, rolling them into tiny balls with his tongue. Finally, give each player a straw. Aiming ONLY at the target, load one spitball (or two, or three!) and blow them out! Keep score, adding up the points of each spitball that actually sticks! Never blow the spit wads at someone else!

100

50

30

thhht!

thhht!

thhht!

25

WATER BALLOON VOLLEYBALL

Form several teams. Team members each hold on to the sides of an old bed sheet or large beach towel. Work together to toss a water balloon to the other team. Keep score, if you want, as you would in regular volleyball matches.

ICE FISHING

Ahead of time fill several large buckets with ice water and marbles. Hide the buckets until time to play. Divide your friends into teams. Everyone removes their shoes and socks. Explain that in this relay race, each team member runs to the bucket, puts his bare foot into the water, pulls out as many marbles as possible on just one try using only toes, places the marbles in a container, and runs back to the team. The next player repeats. Of course, leave out the detail about ice water! The team that pulls the most marbles from the ice water is the winner.

ICE MELT

Ahead of time, fill several half-gallon milk containers with water and freeze. Add a toy action figure to each container. To play, give each team one block of ice with the carton removed. The first team to rescue the action figure by melting their block of ice using only their hands is the winner. Consider allowing team members to use their feet and other body parts, too—but this can be, well, a little gross! Another option is to melt the ice by pouring warm water over the ice block.

NOSE GUM

On a large piece of poster board draw a bull's-eye target. Tape the poster board to a clean wall. Give each player a piece of gum to chew for a few minutes. Blindfold one player at a time and spin them around. Instruct the player to take the gum out of his mouth, stick it to his nose, and then try to stick the gum to the target. Whoever gets the closest to the bull's-eye is the winner.

GUM SCULPTURES

Give each of your friends two or three pieces of bubble gum, an index card, and a toothpick. Let them chew the gum for several minutes. Each player then designs a sculpture with the bubble gum using the toothpick as a tool.

TOE PAINTING

Instead of finger painting, try toe painting! With adult help and supervision, hang a large piece of paper, white paper tablecloth or even a bed sheet on a wall. Be sure to use a drop cloth, too, if you do this inside the house. Kids dip their toes into pie pans or small plastic containers of different color paints. Watercolors or acrylic paints will work well. Divide your friends into teams and award prizes for the most creative, funniest, and scariest paintings. Have a container of warm soapy water and towels nearby to wash and dry each artist's toes!

LOST EYEBALLS

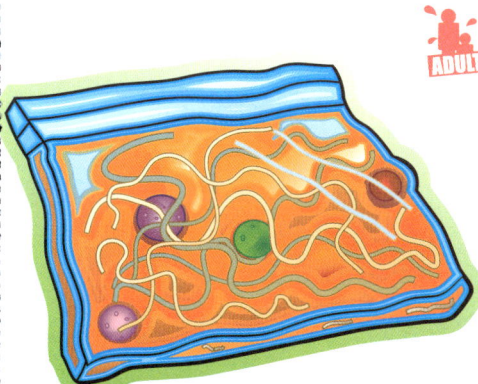

The lost eyeballs are really marbles! Place the marbles in a medium-size plastic storage container. Fill the container with cooked spaghetti noodles doctored up with red food coloring and a small amount of cooking oil. Players take turns searching for the lost eyeballs using only their bare feet.

SQUISH PAINTING

Put a small amount of ketchup and/or mustard inside a large zip-lock sandwich or storage bag. Squeeze out the air and tightly seal the bag. Lay the bag flat, and spread the contents evenly. Draw on the bag with your fingers. Smooth over the bag to erase the drawing. What other mixtures can you place in the bag? Try pudding!

29

RUBBERBAND BALL

To make your own bouncy ball, pinch together the ends of a single rubber band and tie it into a loose double knot. Wrap and twist a second band around the knot repeatedly, until it is taut. Continue adding rubber bands one at a time until the ball is as large as you like, or you run out of bands. You also can speed along the process by covering an inner core of wadded-up newspaper or aluminum foil with rubber bands.

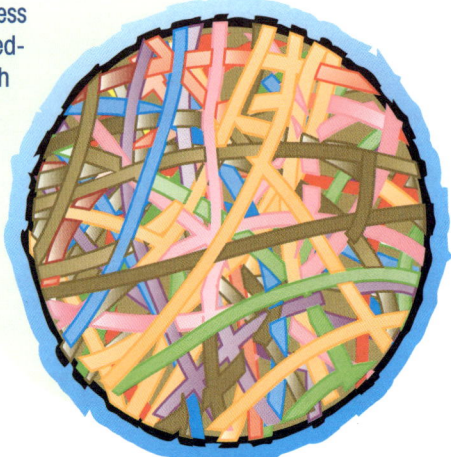

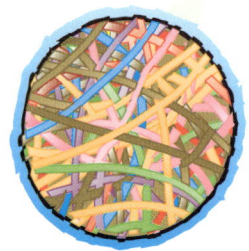

ALIEN INVASION

Okay, so they haven't really come from outer space to take over the world. These one-of-a-kind aliens are still fun to make!

You'll need:
- Balloons
- Cardboard, poster board
- Markers
- Scissors

To make each alien, first make its feet or base: cut out a heart or butterfly shape from poster board or cardboard. Draw on shoes or toes with markers, crayons, or paint. When done, cut a 1/2-inch slit between the heels. Blow up a balloon for each pair of feet and knot the end. Using markers, carefully draw the alien's face and body directly on the balloon. Slip the knotted end of the balloon into the slit between the feet. Stand your alien balloons around the room, or place them where unsuspecting friends will find them.

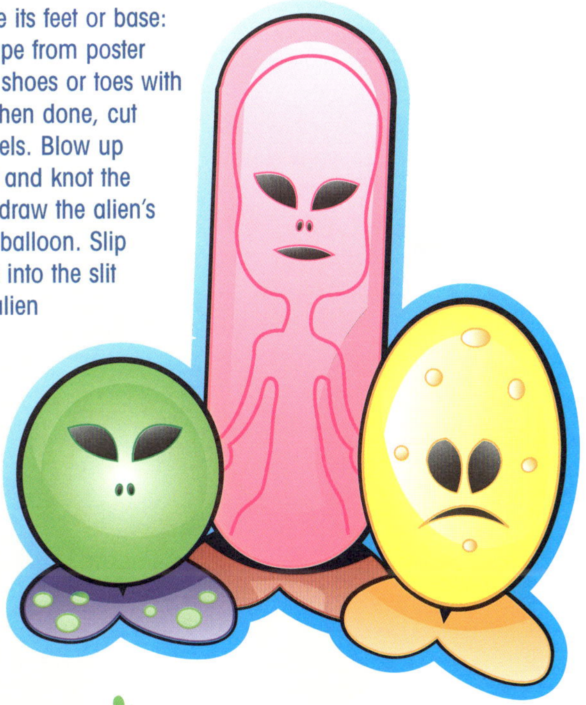

GUMDROP CONSTRUCTION PROJECT

Empty a bag of gumdrops, set out a package of toothpicks, and start to build!
Begin making and combining triangles and squares. Experiment and discover
what formations are sturdier and stronger. The candies will dry out and
crumble—so don't plan on saving the creations! Here's another great idea—
demolish the project with a Gumdrop Eating Contest!

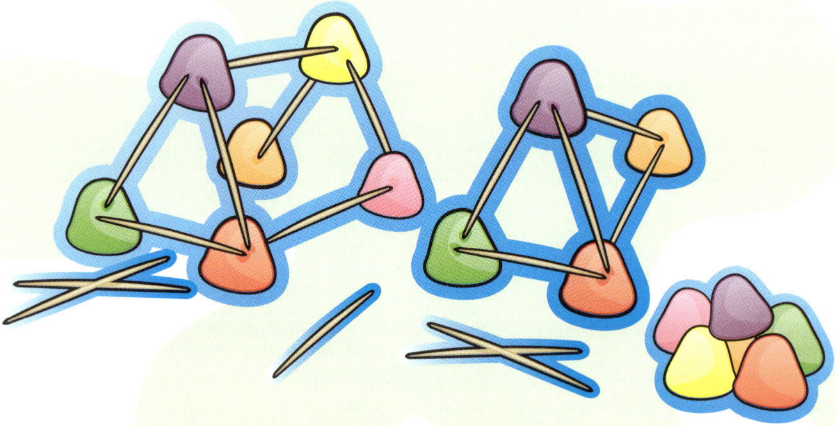

GRUESOME MONSTER HEADS

These shrunken apple heads may take some time, but they're guaranteed to be a scream!

You'll need:

- Peeled apples
- Small paring knife
- Supplies for making hair and facial features— yarn, beads, feathers, dried beans, rice, pasta, and toothpicks
- Craft sticks
- Cups or mugs

With adult supervision, carefully carve eyes, nose, and a mouth into each peeled apple. Don't worry if the carvings aren't perfect—this will make the head look even creepier. Poke rice, beans, dried corn, raisins, or pasta into the apple to make facial features and hair. Be creative! When finished, push a craft stick into the bottom of each apple, and prop upright in a cup or mug in a warm, dry place. Make sure the apple is not touching the side of the cup. Visit the monsters-in-progress every few days. When the apple heads begin to turn leathery you can change facial expressions by gently twisting, pushing, pulling, turning, and rearranging items. In a few weeks you'll have really gruesome monster heads.

33

 # SPIDER WEB T-SHIRTS

You'll need:
- An old white t-shirt
- Black dye
- An old bucket
- Rubber bands
- Permanent markers or fabric paint

What to do:
1. Fill a bucket with black dye following the package directions.
2. Lay an old white t-shirt flat on the table. Pull the t-shirt up from the center and put rubber bands around the "wad" of material. Continue pulling up from the center and adding more rubber bands. The more rubber bands you use, the more your shirt will look like a spider's web.
3. Submerge the whole t-shirt in the bucket of black dye. Follow the package directions. The longer you leave the shirt in the dye, the darker your spider's web will become.
4. Remove the t-shirt from the dye, carefully wring out the excess water, and lay the shirt flat on the floor or table. Allow the shirt to dry completely before removing the rubber bands.
5. Use a permanent marker or fabric paint to draw your spider in its web.

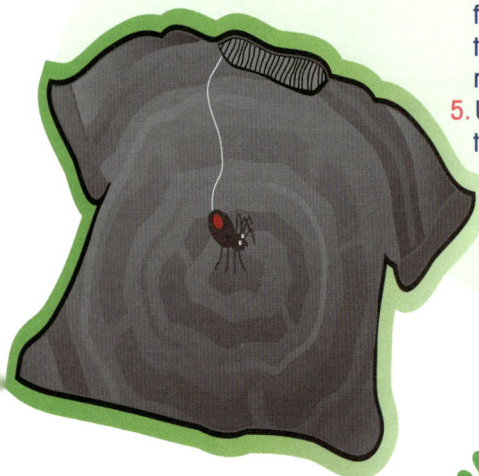

FOIL MASK

You'll need:
- Heavy-duty aluminum foil
- Scissors
- Permanent markers

Cut a 24-by-12-inch piece of heavy-duty aluminum foil. Fold the foil into a 12-inch square. Working together with a friend, press the foil onto your friend's face, making sure to mold it over his cheekbones, nose, lips, and eye sockets. Carefully pull the mask away. Now, have your friend mold your face mask. Use scissors to cut eye, nose, and mouth holes. Add colorful details with a permanent marker, pressing down gently.

SUN CATCHERS

Collect soft, colorless plastic lids from coffee cans and margarine tubs. Draw the outline of a creature or geometric shape with a black permanent marker. Carefully cut out the shape with scissors. Completely fill in the shape with colored permanent markers. When the design is finished, punch a hole in the top of the shape and tie a loop of string or thread. Hang your sun catcher from the top of a window or string a few together to make a mobile.

35

THE IMPORTANT PAPERS

The setting can be either a king or a boss in his office who instructs an assistant to bring royal or important papers. Your friend runs in with a stack of papers. The king or boss is quite upset, tosses the papers aside, and demands that the assistant bring him his really important papers. Other people bring in other stacks of papers one at a time. The king throws them aside and becomes more and more upset, angrily insisting that he have his important papers. At last someone comes in with a roll of bathroom tissue. The king knights or the boss promotes the assistant, thanking him profusely before running off the stage in visible relief.

STRONG COFFEE

Set a large pan of dirty water in the center of the stage. You and three of your friends each walk one at a time to the pan, carrying a coffee mug, dip the mug in, bring it up to your lips for a drink, and say:

1st friend: "This coffee is getting worse!"

2nd friend: "This tea is getting worse!"

3rd friend: "This chocolate is getting worse!"

The fourth friend, walks to pan, dips his hands in and takes out a pair of dirty, wet socks. As he wrings them out he says, "I thought that would get them clean!"

THE LITTLE GREEN BALL

The first friend enters and says, "Oh no I've lost it!" He then starts to search around on the floor. The second friend comes in and asks what the first person is looking for. The first person replies that he has lost his little green ball. Both continue searching the floor. Several more friends come on and are told about the lost little green ball. Even members of the audience can be persuaded to join in the search. The key is to be melodramatic, exaggerating movements and words. After enough time has been dragged out, the first person sticks a finger up his nose and says, "Don't worry! I can make another one!" YUK!!!!!

37

THE LEGEND OF HERBERT SMEAR...

ADULT

Tell ghost stories in the dark and pass around the bowls of the items below. Another option is to blindfold your friends, have them sit in a circle on the floor, and pass the body parts around the circle for each to feel as you tell the horrific tale.

Brains: An overcooked head of cauliflower

Eyes: Olives or peeled grapes

Live Worms: Gummy worms—not as scary though

Intestines: Soggy marshmallows, strung together

Zombie Hair: Dried corn silk from ears of corn

Barf/Vomit: Chunky salsa and canned corn mixed together

Pranks & Skits

Teeth: Dried popcorn kernels

Decaying Flesh: Mashed potatoes topped with instant potato flakes, add coloring

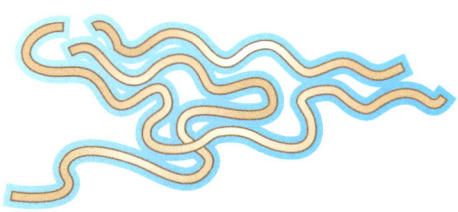

Veins: Cooked spaghetti

Maggots: Cooked mini pasta shells, or rice

Breaking Bones: Fresh crisp celery or dog biscuits

Scrambled Brains: Lumpy cottage cheese

39

PUPPY IN THE BOX

Props: A cardboard box, and a stuffed dog or animal.

Announcer:	This scene takes place on the street outside a grocery store. *(Several friends are gathered, chatting outside the store.)*
Michael:	*(Enters holding the box)* Hi guys! Would you please hold this box for me while I go into the store? *(Exits)*
Nathan:	I wonder what's in the box?
Jason:	I don't know, but something yellow is leaking out!
Bob:	*(Rubs finger against the bottom of box then licks finger.)* Hmmm, it tastes like lemon soda.
Nathan:	*(Also rubs box and licks finger.)* No. I think it's more like chicken soup.
Michael:	*(Returns, looks into the box.)* Oh, you naughty puppy!

DANDRUFF FLAKES

Put small amounts of cornstarch or finely crushed instant oatmeal in your hair. Be sure to scratch it out for all your friends to see!

GOT CHANGE?

Superglue several coins to the sidewalk or any spot that has a lot of people walking nearby. Make sure it's an appropriate place, then watch people break fingernails to get the coins.

41

GROSS SONGS

and annoying *kids love to sing!*

TAKE A SHOWER, PLEASE!

Put a rubber band around the handle of the kitchen sink sprayer when nobody's looking. This automatically keeps the nozzle in spray mode. Make sure the nozzle is pointing up and outward. The next person to use the sink will take a shower!

ALIEN MILK

Serve your favorite breakfast cereal, but add green food coloring to the milk container before it's poured. This works best with an opaque milk container—one you can't see through! The looks on your friends' faces should be priceless.

Gross
Recipes

EGG EYEBALLS

So you're not a brain surgeon! How about an eye doctor? You and your friends will have plenty of patients with these eye-popping treats.

Ingredients:
- 6 Eggs, hard-cooked, cooled and peeled
- 6-oz whipped cream cheese
- 12 green olives stuffed with pimentos
- Ketchup
- Toothpick

Ask an adult to hardboil several eggs. When the eggs have cooled, remove the shell, and cut the eggs in half widthwise. Remove the yolks and fill the hole with cream cheese. Press an olive into each cream cheese eyeball, pimento up, for an eerie green iris and red pupil. Dip a toothpick into ketchup and draw broken blood vessels in the cream cheese!

43

 **BOOGERS ON A STICK**

The name says it all! Kids will love them!

> Ingredients:
> • 8-ounce jar of processed cheese spread
> • 3 or 4 drops green food coloring
> • 3 dozen pretzel sticks

Ask an adult to melt the processed cheese spread in the microwave according to jar directions. Allow the cheese to cool slightly in the jar. Carefully stir in green food coloring, using just enough to turn the cheese a pale, snot green color. To form boogers, dip and twist the tip of each pretzel stick into the cheese, lift out, wait twenty seconds, then dip again. When the cheese lumps reach a boogerish size, set boogered pretzels on wax paper to cool.

SEWER SLURPIES

Disgusting? Yes, but tasty too! You and your friends can cool off some with this sweet-tasting ice cream beverage!

Ingredients:
- Chocolate chip ice cream
- Chocolate syrup
- Club soda

Let the ice cream sit at room temperature until it's easy to scoop. Fill tall glasses halfway with the ice cream goop. Squeeze several tablespoons of chocolate syrup into each glass. Slowly fill glasses with club soda and serve with a straw and long spoon.

45

STRAWBERRY RETCH

Not much tastes better than a tall, cool glass of Strawberry Retch on a hot, summer day.

Ingredients:
- 3-oz package strawberry gelatin
- 40 ice cubes
- 2 cans of strawberry soda

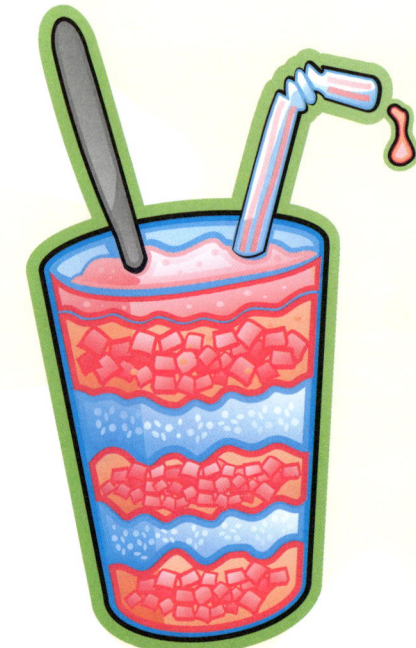

Ask an adult to prepare the strawberry gelatin according to the package directions. Pour the gelatin into a shallow pan and chill about three hours. When set, make as many cuts as possible across the length and width of the gelatin, forming tiny cubes. Set the gelatin aside. Next, with an adult's help, crush ice cubes in a blender. Spoon alternating layers of crushed ice and gelatin pieces into tall glasses, filling them about 2" away from tops. Slowly pour strawberry soda into each glass until full and stir gently. Serve Strawberry Retch with long spoons and straws.

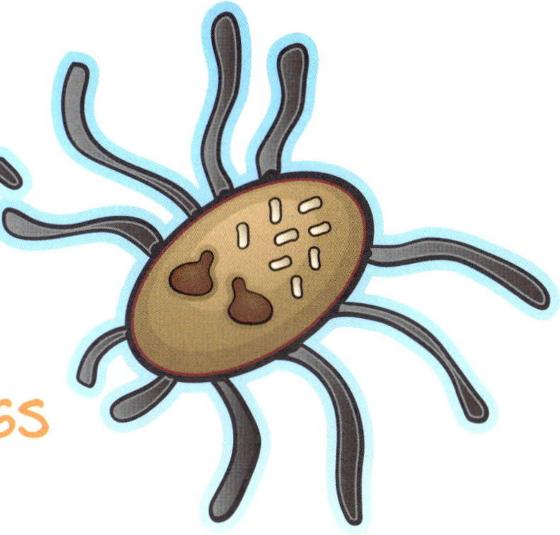

CHOCOLATE COVERED BUGS

ADULT

Ingredients:
- Red-licorice whips
- Soft caramel candies
- Chocolate chips
- Optional: colored sprinkles, candies, coconut, sliced almonds

Wash your hands before making these delicious sweet tasting chocolate bugs. First, cut the licorice whips into small pieces and set them aside. Unwrap the caramels and flatten each one into a small oval. Press the small pieces of licorice onto each flattened caramel to make bug legs. Top each bug with a second caramel and seal together by pressing the edges. Put each bug on a baking sheet lined with waxed paper.

With adult help, melt the chocolate chips in a microwave-safe bowl. Microwave on High about 1 minute. Stir. Then microwave on High 1 minute longer. Remove the chocolate from the microwave and stir until melted. Spoon melted chocolate over each caramel. Decorate the bugs with nuts, candies, coconut, or sprinkles.

 # SPIDER GUTS

Slice into this gooey cake for a disgusting surprise!

Ingredients:
- 1 Basic cake mix
- 1 Package of green gelatin, prepared according to package directions
- Black frosting—available at craft supply stores or make your own by adding blue food coloring to chocolate frosting
- Black licorice sticks or whips
- Large green gumdrops

Mix the cake batter according to package directions. Ask an adult to bake the cake in a bowl. Once the cake has baked and cooled, remove it from the mold. To make the spider's body, cut the cake in half horizontally. Scoop out a hole in each half. Fill the hole with the green gelatin. Put both halves of the cake back together. Frost it black and arrange on a serving platter. Add licorice whip legs, gumdrop eyes, and candy body markings. When the cake is cut into, it will ooze green guts!